Top 100 Cruising Tips for Beginners

by Katrina Abiasi

Top 100 Cruising Tips for Beginners.

Copyright © 2012 by Katrina Abiasi. All rights reserved. No part of this book may be reproduced in any form without permission in writing from the author.

Disclaimer: Any content or information in "Top 100 Cruising Tips for Beginners" is for informational and educational purposes only and any use thereof is solely at your own risk. The author bears no responsibility thereof.

Introduction

A properly planned and executed cruise can be one of the best vacation values on the market, not to mention a fun and unforgettable memory for you and your loved ones. However, it is also possible to waste thousands on a poorly planned cruise. In this eBook, we will go over 100 of the best tips for not only planning your cruise, but booking your cruise and getting a good value aboard your cruise. We will also go over safety aboard the ship and special tips for families and couples.

This book is designed for those who have no knowledge of how to plan a cruise, so if you have already begun planning your cruise you may find some of the information a bit repetitive. However, this book will walk you through every aspect of your cruise- from the earliest stages of planning to the very last moments of your trip. There are even a couple of bonus tips for booking your second cruise. Any first time cruiser can learn something from this eBook.

If you want to have an amazing cruise vacation, you need only read on.

Chapter 1: Tips for Planning and Booking Your Cruise

1) Decide the length of your trip.

You can take a cruise almost anywhere, but deciding on a trip length will narrow down your destination choices considerably.

2) Decide what activities you'd like to do on your trip.

This will also narrow down your destination options. For instance, if you plan on visiting beaches or wish to participate in water sports, you will probably be taking a Caribbean or South Pacific cruise. If you wish to visit historical sites or museums, you will want to take a European cruise.

3) Pick a cabin where you will be comfortable.

Experts recommend a cabin in the middle of the ship on a lower deck for the smoothest ride. There are also some ships that now have rooms with balconies, which is something else to consider. Make sure to book early for the biggest selection.

4) Decide on a dress code.

Many cruise lines have semi-formal dress, so if you aren't up for that you might want to stick to a more casual ship.

5) Set a budget.

It is extremely easy to go over-budget on a cruise (or any vacation for that matter). Before doing the bulk of your planning, you need to set a strict budget for your trip so you do not overspend before you even set sail. Hint: You'll need at least $100 per person, per day.

6) Get a travel agent.

After you have decided the basics, like the length of your trip, your destination, who will be going, etc., it would be best to get a travel agent if it is your first time cruising.

7) Make a basic itinerary.

At this stage, you just need to decide what events you would like to take part in (onshore and on the boat). Setting a schedule is not only helpful for time management- it also helps you to not go over-budget while on your trip.

8) Make sure all your IDs are up to date (same goes for everyone traveling with you).

You will need at least one proof of ID at all times when traveling. Each cruise line has different policies on what form of ID you need, so make sure you have the proper identification, and make sure it's up to date. If a passport is required, check this early. It can take more than six months to re-register your passport.

9) If you are traveling abroad, check to see if you need any visas to the country/countries you are traveling to.

If you do, contact your travel agent about acquiring those.

10) Make sure you keep a balanced budget between now and the time you set sail.

Any vacation is a substantial investment. Make sure you pace yourself as far as finances are concerned.

11) If you are traveling in the winter, consider flying into your port city early.

Winter weather can sometimes interfere with travel plans with snow canceling or delaying flights. You may want to fly into your port city a day or two early in order to avoid missing the boat.

12) If you are traveling in good weather, make sure you give yourself enough time to get from the plane or car to the boat.

One of the easiest mistakes to make when booking your first cruise is to book your flight too close to the departure time of the boat. Make sure you give yourself enough travel time. Keep in mind that you also have to be on deck an average of two hours and thirty minutes prior to departure. This needs to be factored into your travel time as well.

13) Don't bundle.

Cruises often offer pre-packaged flight and cruise "deals." Usually these offers will not save you money. In fact, by purchasing one of these offers, you may wind up spending more than you would by purchasing airfare, cruise room and board separately. Make sure you compare prices or ask your travel agent before purchasing everything.

14) Make sure your cabin isn't under a well-travelled area.

Some areas are loud and will create noise in the rooms below even in the early morning hours. Make sure you haven't booked one of these rooms by checking the deck plans online.

15) Book during January-March.

Cruise ships offer many of their best deals at this time, as this is when they make over a third of their annual sales. Book during this time for the best deals with the best perks.

Chapter 2: Tips for Packing for Your Cruise

16) Consider bringing some extra bottled drinks.

The easiest way to spend extra money on a cruise is by purchasing expensive drinks on the boat (or on shore). If you are always with a bottled drink in hand, definitely make sure you pack some for your cruise. Be careful though; some cruise ships don't allow you to bring your own beverages onboard. Check your ship's policies before packing anything.

17) Sunscreen, sunscreen, sunscreen!

There is no excuse for not bringing sunscreen on your cruise. Even if you are going on a cruise in a colder climate, you will still probably be outside a fair amount of the time. No matter the climate or the weather, sunscreen is necessary for preventing skin cancer and other health concerns.

18) Pack some basic first-aid and medicine.

Pack a few band-aids, wipes, pain killers, some cold medicine, and some other simple supplies. This will save you some trips to the pharmacy or infirmary if you should happen to get sick or get a small injury. These supplies will be expensive on the boat, so packing them beforehand will save money, too.

19) If you are used to having an alarm clock next to you when you sleep, you may wish to bring one with you on your cruise.

A typical cruise cabin does not include an alarm clock.

20) Bring some extra space.

Chances are you will need some extra room in your cabin for storage. Find out as much as you can about the floor plan of your room. You may be able to bring plastic bins for under your bed or hang a storage unit on the back of your door.

21) You'll need a power strip.

This isn't essential if you don't plan on bringing a lot of electronic equipment with you, but chances are, if you plan on bringing the amount of electronics you use every day (most of us use a lot) you are going to need the extra outlets. A typical cruise cabin is usually only equipped with one outlet.

22) Minimize your luggage by finding clothing pieces you can mix and match.

Don't pack a lot of pieces that you can only wear once. This tip applies more to women than men, but men should keep this in mind as well. Also, as we mentioned in the last chapter, make sure you check your ship's dress code before packing.

23) You may want to consider bringing a lanyard with you.

Having your IDs, credit card, traveler's checks and other important items around your neck at all times is much more convenient than having to dig through a purse or wallet to find them. You will have to present multiple forms of ID many times throughout your trip, so having a lanyard is a smart idea for that use alone.

24) Bring some low-tech entertainment for beach days or days when you wish to sit out on the boat.

Books, crossword puzzles or word searches, magazines, or other easy to pack items are always appropriate. Binoculars are also a good idea if you are going on a cruise with a lot of wildlife.

25) Backpacks or totes are useful for carrying your daily-use items around the ship (sunscreen, book, towel if you are swimming, etc).

For women, consider bringing something larger than your purse to carry both your purse items and daily-use items.

26) Bring some air freshener.

Most cabins don't have fans, and they really are smaller than you think. Air freshener will make a huge difference if you have to share a bathroom with anyone.

27) Pack some small magnets.

Many cabin doors are metal, so you will be able to hang important papers to them. You may want to hang up the daily newsletter, which lists the activities and meals for the day, as well as the dress code and stops if there are any.

28) Save room for souvenirs.

You definitely want to leave some room in your bag for souvenirs. Even if you don't think you are going to buy anything, definitely leave some room in your bag (or even bring an extra bag) just in case. This is especially important for tropical cruises, where luau wear and tropical wear becomes more and more fashionable as time progresses.

29) Remember to label your luggage!

It might seem like a no brainer, but don't forget to put your name, address and phone number on your luggage. It's easy to forget to do this when you are packing for a totally new experience.

30) Bring a reusable water bottle.

Water bottles are expensive (not to mention wasteful for the environment). Bring a reusable water bottle and use it for the entirety of your trip. You will be provided with ice in your room and you can get water from your sink.

Chapter 3: Tips for Saving Money on Your Cruise

31) Book your own day trips.

If you book your offshore excursions on your own rather than through the cruise line, you will save a lot of money. Day trips through the cruise line will have inflated prices, and you will most likely be able to plan the same activities the cruise line offers for a much lower price.

32) Bring your own wine.

Many cruise lines allow you to bring a bottle or two of wine on board. Wine on the ship will be offered at a much higher price than offshore (sometimes the price will be doubled on the ship) so bringing your own wine is a must if you plan on having any on your trip- just make sure the cruise line allows it.

33) Don't use the spa onboard.

Most cruise lines offer spa discounts when you reach land, so if you plan on hitting the spa, wait until the ship is in port. Just watch out for the sales pitch that will most likely follow your spa treatments. Spa employees often work on commission, so they will probably push their products on you when you finish your treatment. However, don't feel obliged to purchase anything unless it's something you really like AND it fits in your budget.

34) Book your cruise very far in advance or less than two months before departure.

If you are planning on traveling on a popular route or line, make sure you book early. Booking this far in advance may also get you an early bird discount. On the other hand, for those with flexible schedules, booking your cruise late should also ensure you a lower rate.

35) If you are a bit of a risk taker, opt to take a Caribbean cruise during hurricane season.

This will ensure you an extremely low rate, sometimes less than half of a regular cruise rate.

You can always get travel insurance if you're nervous about issues with the weather.

36) See if you can pre-reserve any meals.

Some cruise lines offer discounted rates for meals that are booked far in advance.

37) Stick to juice rather than soda, alcohol or bottled water to save money.

While you almost always have to pay for bottled water or soda, many cruise lines now offer juice for free. If you are traveling with children and want to save money, try having them stick with juice.

38) Make sure you allot some space in your budget for tips.

You are expected to tip your cabin steward and waiters. These people live off of their tips, so make sure you tip adequately. As a rule of thumb, you are expected to tip about $10 per day- $3.50 for the steward, $5.50 to be split between the dining room waiter and assistant waiter, and $1 for the bistro service waiter and cooks. Tips for drinks from the bar are automatically added to your bill, so don't worry about tipping the bartender (although feel free to tip extra if he or she does an extra special job!). Other crew, such as the bellmen or the maître, should be tipped when they help you.

39) Depending on the length of your trip, you may want to bring laundry supplies.

There will be laundry facilities on the ship, but they might be expensive to use. Bringing products like wrinkle spray, Febreeze spray or stain remover will save you a lot of money if you find that you need to wear your clothes more than once. You can also hand wash your clothes in your sink if you bring a travel sized bottle of detergent.

40) If you have to use the Internet, try to wait until you reach port.

Many ships charge a very high per-minute fee for Internet access. Wait until you can get free access on shore.

Chapter 4: Tips for Families

41) There are many cruise lines aimed at families, some of the best being Disney Cruise Line, Family Cruise Lines, Princess Cruises and Royal Caribbean International.

42) Look at what is included in the cruise price.

A cruise may seem like a good value until you get on board and see that everything you want to do costs extra. One important thing to consider is babysitting facilities. Ships vary on whether or not they charge for babysitting, so if this is an important factor in your trip it is definitely something to consider when choosing a cruise.

43) Consider getting a drink package.

This isn't recommended if you aren't traveling in a large family, but if you are with a few kids who are always on the go and need fuel, you'll definitely want to consider a drink package. Disney Cruise Line offers unlimited complimentary soda and juice machine access around the clock, included in the cruise price. However, it is the only known line to do so.

44) If you have babies or toddlers, make sure there are plenty of stops during your cruise.

They are bound to get squirmy staying on the ship for days at a time, even if there are activities on board to keep them busy.

45) Make sure you bring your own diapers if you have a baby who still uses them.

The same rule goes for baby food and formula.

46) Check to see that there is appropriate kids' programming on board, and make sure your kids are at or above the minimum age requirement to get in to the programs.

Make sure there is enough going on that your kids will be occupied for the entire duration of your cruise. You may only send them to one program, but it's still good to know that there are options if you need them.

47) Make sure you take time changes into consideration before booking your cruise.

If your kids have a very rigid sleep schedule, there is a very high chance that they'll be affected by the time change and jet lag. You may want to stick to a local cruise when traveling with young children.

48) Get walkie-talkies.

If you have older kids who are more independent, they are going to want to be off on their own. Get walkie-talkies as a way of staying connected with everyone without getting extra charges on your cell phone.

49) If you are traveling in a very large group, check to see if you can get a free cabin.

Most cruise lines will throw in a free cabin for groups of 15 or more people.

50) Keep in mind that your luggage may not be delivered to your ship until several hours after you arrive.

Make sure you pack enough in your carry-on bag to be able to start your trip before your luggage arrives.

Chapter 5: Tips for Couples

51) Don't stay up late the first night.

You will probably be really tempted to explore everything the ship has to offer the first night out, but don't do that. You will be much better off starting your trip relaxed and refreshed the second morning.

52) Unpack your things together.

There are so many places to unpack your things in your cabin, and you may not remember where you put something. If you unpack with your spouse or significant other, you will have a point of reference in the event that you misplace something.

53) Make sure you are friendly with the other cruisers.

A big part of a cruise is meeting new people, so expect to meet some new pals on your cruise. You may not meet any lifelong friends, but you should be able to easily find other couples to enjoy activities or meals with.

52) You may want to ask the maître'd to assign you to a large table for dinner.

This will help you get to know some of the other passengers easily. Also make sure you go to the later dinner if there is more than one sitting.

If you go to the earlier sitting, you may be shooed out in order to set up for the next sitting.

55) As we mentioned in the last section, you may want to bring a pair of walkie- talkies for easier communication if you and your partner split up.

It's also a smart idea to bring post-it notes. If you have to remind your partner of something while they are out of the cabin, you can easily leave them a post-it note. You can also use post-its as a way to ask the steward for more towels, soap, etc.

56) Decide whether or not you wish to go on a more "adult-friendly" cruise.

If so, have your travel agent suggest a cruise that will be more catered to adult interests.

57) Familiarize yourselves with your cabin early.

Cruise cabins are a lot smaller than a standard hotel room, so you and your partner will want to get comfortable moving around in your cabin together. This will help you avoid a lot of bumping and tripping when getting ready for dinner and other activities.

58) Do not try to do every activity the first time you cruise.

You will simply wear yourself out, and maybe even turn yourself off to future cruises. Just pick a maximum of one activity a day. This will help you enjoy the cruise to its fullest.

59) Bring a camera with you and use it.

There will be a professional photographer offering to snap photos of you and your partner at every turn, but the photos will cost you. Bring your own camera and people will be happy to snap a photo of you in the same spots and poses as the pros.

60) It may seem obvious, but pick a time when kids are less likely to be onboard.

This means that it would be best to go during the school year. Also make sure you aren't booking your cruise during "Kids Sail Free" days, which many cruise lines now offer.

Chapter 6: Safety Tips for Your Cruise

61) Make sure you pay attention to the muster drills scheduled during your cruise where you will be instructed on how to handle different emergency situations.

It may seem like it will never happen to you, but you can never be too prepared for a crisis situation that you never expected to encounter. If you should happen to run into an emergency situation, crew members will probably be too busy to assist you personally, which is all the more reason to pay attention.

62) Consider travel insurance.

Travel insurance policies cover anything from misplaced or stolen luggage to medical expenses. The longer your trip, the more likely it is that you'll need insurance.

63) Go over your current health insurance plan.

If you are traveling abroad, make sure your insurance plan covers injuries and medical care abroad. In the case that you have to be checked into a hospital overseas, you want to make sure you're covered.

64) Don't bring your most expensive jewelry, watches or purses.

Those can be left at home. It is too easy for them to be lost or stolen on a cruise, so if you value them at all, don't bring them along.

65) Be safe about offshore excursions.

Ask crew members about parts of town that are off limits. You should also research cruise stops online or in travel books before booking any tours or trips.

66) Try to travel in groups of two or more whenever possible.

This will make you less likely to get lost or get into a dangerous situation.

67) Do not hang anything from the fire sprinkler heads in your cabin.

Similarly, do not have an open flame in your cabin (such as an aroma candle).

68) Scan your passport and have it on an easily accessed file so you can find it in the event that you lose yours.

On European cruises it is common that your passport is withheld by the crew for the duration of the cruise so they can easily clear customs, so it is good to have another copy on hand in case yours is lost or stolen.

69) Feeling seasick? Try eating a green apple.

An alternative is to peel an orange, hold the rind to your nose and inhale. Candied ginger is another natural remedy (some ships even offer it with after dinner mints).

70) Pack a small waterproof bag in your luggage.

Make sure that you can easily secure it on your body in the event that you need to evacuate the ship. That way you won't have to leave all of your valuables behind.

Chapter 7: Ten Cruise Myths Debunked

71) Cruises are not all-inclusive.

In most instances, the basic price of a cruise only includes room and board. You are also welcome to use the basic amenities on board such as the swimming pool and lounge chairs. Anything else, from the gym to the food to the activities, will be extra. However, you can find creative ways to spend less money on a cruise if you wish to. We've been listing tips throughout to do just that.

72) You will not get seasick.

One of the biggest myths about cruising is that you will get seasick on the boat. This is most likely not the case. Cruise ships are extremely smooth and stable nowadays, so seasickness is a rarity. However, if you are still worried about it, there are plenty of over the counter medicines made specifically to relieve seasickness or nausea.

73) The ship will not be too crowded.

It may seem unfathomable that a cruise ship with thousands of passengers wouldn't be overly crowded. In fact, cruises are no more or less crowded than any other vacation destination. Even the biggest ships have plenty of space per passenger, and cruise workers are trained in crowd control should crowds become a problem.

74) You will be safe on your cruise.

A common cruise myth is that cruise ships are unsafe. This is far from the truth. Tens of millions of people cruise every year, and the crime rate is very low. Accidents are also a rarity. To ensure a safe trip, follow our safety tips in the previous chapter.

75) There is plenty to do on a cruise ship.

Cruise ships are sometimes thought of as a "boring" vacation. This is the complete opposite of the truth. There are endless classes, clubs, sports activities and restaurants to occupy your time- and that's just aboard the ship! Once you stop at a port, you will have even more activities to look forward to. There will be more than enough to occupy your time on your cruise. It will be impossible to get bored.

76) Cruises are about more than just eating and drinking.

While fine dining can be a big part of any cruise, it doesn't have to be. Cruises offer lower priced or lower calorie options for anyone looking for an alternative menu.

77) Cruises are not as scheduled as you think.

One thing that often steers people away from cruising is that they believe that a cruise vacation is too scheduled. This is no longer the case. While some cruises still have scheduled dinner seating, there is usually more than one option, and there is almost always more than one restaurant in case you miss dinner. There are also myriad options of activities for you to do throughout your trip. There is no way you should feel restricted by a schedule.

78) Cruises are not just for the elderly.

This was true in the past, and is still somewhat true on some ships. However, according to the Cruise Lines International Association, the majority of cruisers today are between 48 and 59 years old. Younger passengers (25-39) and older passengers (60+) are tied for second place.

79) Cruises are not just for party people.

Cruises are actually marketed towards multi-generational families, not partiers. It's not as if you won't find them on a cruise ship, but they will definitely be in the minority.

80) You shouldn't worry about getting sick.

That doesn't mean it won't happen, but you shouldn't worry about it. You've probably seen reports about the Norovirus on cruise ships, and maybe it scared you. Don't let it. Norovirus is more common than the common cold, and it has similar symptoms. It is brought about by someone with the bug leaving germs on a doorknob or handrail and someone else picking up the germs and passing it along. There is no certainty someone with the bug (or any contagious disease) will or will not be on your ship, but to be safe and prevent catching it, wash your hands frequently.

Chapter 8: Tips for Cruise Dining

81) Order and eat what you like.

You may be served a four or five course meal some nights. You don't have to eat every course. Eat what you want and leave what you don't want on your plate. Furthermore, make sure you take note of what you like and order a second helping if you wish. Menus usually don't repeat, so if you like something, enjoy it while you can.

82) If you don't like your seat, move.

If you are uncomfortable at your table, you don't have to stay there. Request a seat change from the maître'd.

83) If you *do* like your seat, move.

If possible, try sitting in a different seat at your table each night. That way it will be easier to have different conversations with different members of the table each night.

84) Get to know your waiter.

If you give your waiter personal attention, you will get the same back. Call your waiter by his or her name, greet them hello, etc. If they speak a different language than you, learn some simple phrases. This will go a long way.

85) Most ships serve local cuisine.

For example, you'll probably be eating Caribbean food on a Caribbean cruise. The point here is, if you aren't into a certain type of food, you may want to stay away from that cruise. However, there will always be secondary options for those who need them.

86) You will gain weight on a cruise if you aren't careful.

You will be able to get food and drink 24 hours a day, and it's not necessarily anything that's good for you. If you are concerned about gaining weight on your cruise, go for the healthy options that are available on most cruise menus.

87) Have an early morning? Get breakfast in bed.

If you have an early morning excursion, order room service the night before. You'll avoid lines at the buffet and potentially missing your outing.

88) Check out your dining options on land before spending money.

It might be more worth your time and money to skip eating out while at port. Instead, book some room service while ashore. It'll be ready and waiting for you in your room (and still hot if you call at the right time) when you return.

89) Having a birthday? Tell the crew.

If you are celebrating a birthday, anniversary or other special occasion, the ship will usually offer you a complimentary cake for the occasion. You can even have a private party if you wish. Just make sure to alert your travel agent in advance.

90) Eat earlier if you are traveling with kids.

The earlier seating option is usually around 6PM.

Chapter 9: Odds and Ends

91) Some cruise lines give free passage for those qualified to teach a class or give lectures.

Call your travel agent or contact the cruise line of your choice for details.

92) Many cruise lines offer automatic upgrades from indoor cabins to an ocean view room.

Watch the cruise line's website or have your travel agent keep an eye on it for you.

93) Ask for a print-out of your bill the day before you hit shore.

If you do this, you will avoid long lines at check-out and be able to resolve any problems with your bill earlier than the other passengers.

94) Go on a ship tour.

Try to go on a ship tour close to departure time. This will help you get to know the ship easier, and you may even get a head start on meeting some fellow passengers if others are on the tour with you.

95) Check if your ship has any theme nights.

Many ships have "theme nights" where you can dress up for dinner or other activities such as the Royal Caribbean's "Masquerade Ball." Other popular theme nights include "Mystery Dinner" theater night or decade themed dress-up dinners.

96) Keep an eye on your kids.

Your kids are your responsibility. This should be left unsaid, but in this sue-crazy time it's necessary to reiterate it. For everyone's (that means you, your children, the other passengers and the cruise employees) safety and enjoyment of the trip, be sure you keep a watchful eye on your children. It's not impossible to be banned from a cruise line for unruly children.

97) Consider the cruise line's mailing list or credit card.

The mailing list will probably get you small perks on your cruise or coupons you can use while on your trip. The credit card, on the other hand, will probably help you save money by racking up points when you use it on your trip. Both are valuable and useful.

98) Check out time is bright and early!

Make sure you have an alarm set for your final day onboard the ship. Check out time is usually very early (between eight and nine in the morning typically), so give yourself ample time to pack your things. Staff is strict about check out time.

99) Be a polite audience member.

If you are viewing a show, the same rules apply as if you were viewing any other show in any other theater. Just because it might be free doesn't mean you can be rude to the performers and other audience members. Make sure you silence your cell phone and don't talk during the performance. If you have to get up during the performance, do so as discreetly as possible.

100) Dress appropriately.

Even if you are on a casual-dress ship, that doesn't mean you should flaunt your PJs for public view. Here's a general rule of thumb: if you wouldn't wear it to the grocery store, don't wear it on deck.

Conclusion

So there you have it- 100 tips for a great first cruise. You will now be able to book your cruise, pack for your cruise, and enjoy your trip like a cruise veteran. Keep in mind that when you book your cruise, you are only booking room and board; *everything* else will most likely be extra- even down to a bottle of water. You also want to keep in mind that you have to pack for cruises differently than other vacations- alarm clocks aren't included in your room for example (and you'll definitely need one!). You'll also want to make sure you pack some extra storage for your cabin. And last but not least- make sure you plan your budget carefully!

So what are you waiting for? Hop on that computer or cell phone and get to booking!

While we're at it, here are a few tips for your second and subsequent cruises:

101) If you book your next cruise while on still onboard your first cruise, you can save.

Cruise lines offer discounts of $175 and up if you deposit with them while still aboard. You can also cancel the deposit and get a full refund, so it's definitely worth it.

102) Ask about past guest discounts when booking your next cruise.

Many cruise lines have discounts for people who have already sailed with them.

Made in the USA
San Bernardino, CA
13 February 2016